Best
Annuals
& Perennials

By Barbara W. Ellis

Neil Soderstrom, Principal Photographer

TYPHOON
MEDIA CORPORATION

Published by:
TYPHOON MEDIA CORPORATION

Best Annuals & Perennials

Best Annuals & Perennials
© TYPHOON MEDIA CORPORATION

Publisher
Simon St. John Bailey

Editor-in-chief
Elaine Evans

Producer, Editor and Principal Photographer
Neil Soderstrom

Prepress
Precision Prep & Press

Photography
All photos by Neil Soderstrom except following:
All-America Selections: 49top
Ball Horticultural Company: 10(Scabiosa & Shasta daisies), 34top, 36both, 39bot, 45bot, 47top, 52top, 62top
Barbara W. Ellis: 7, 9, 13, 19bot3, 33rt, 46bot2, 52bot3, 55both, 56top, 57both, 58, 59bot, 60both, 61top

ISBN 9781600814433
UPC 615269144336

2010

Printed in the United States

Best
Annuals
& Perennials

Part 1: Getting Started

Planning Your Garden   5

Getting Ready to Garden   12

Planting Your Flowers   16

Caring for Your Garden   22

Part 2: Best Flowers for Sun 25

Part 3: Best Flowers for Shade 52

Hardiness Zone Map 64

Part 1: Getting Started

Every gardener dreams of having a gorgeous, colorful garden filled with flowers. The good news is that even if you are a beginning gardener, you can have a yard filled with blooming annuals and perennials. It's no secret that flowers have their own likes and dislikes. Some want sun, while others want shade. I've found that the best way to make a garden thrive, with a minimum of work, is to use plant likes and dislikes to advantage. In this booklet, I explain how you can do just that in creating your own beautiful flower garden.

This features yellow-orange rudbeckia, colorfully leaved coleus, and also blue and red salvia.
Site: Hollandia Nursery & Garden Center, Bethel, CT

Planning Your Garden

In upcoming pages, you'll find my best tips for choosing annuals and perennials that grow well and look pretty together. If you start by learning about your garden site and then choosing flowers that will be happy there, you will be well on your way to success.

Kinds of Flowers

To plan a flower garden, it helps to understand the different types of plants.

Cosmos 'Sonata'

Annuals are the garden's one-hit wonders. They flower almost continuously all season, but need replacing each year. They bloom more than perennial flowers because they don't store food in their roots to survive the winter the way other plants do.

These hardworking plants are commonly described as being either cool- or warm-weather annuals. Cool-weather annuals, such as alyssum, thrive in cool temperatures. They're best for the spring or fall garden. In mild climates, many also can be grown over winter. Warm-weather annuals such as cosmos and marigolds thrive during hot summer weather.

Tender Perennials are routinely killed by frost at season's end. Often grown like annuals, they include zonal geraniums, wax begonias, and coleus. Like annuals, they bloom all summer because they don't store food to survive the winter. Bring these plants indoors before frost, and you can replant them in spring.

Coleus 'Tilt-A-Whirl'

Perennials, also called hardy perennials, live for two or more seasons. Their roots go dormant in fall and resprout in spring. Hostas and daylilies are two popular examples. Perennials grow bigger and produce more flowers every year. Besides returning each year, their root systems can be divided and the divisions transplanted.

Daylily 'Hall's Pink'

Biennials, including hollyhocks and foxgloves, produce leaves the first year and flowers the second. They often self sow, producing new seedlings to replace the old plants.

Hollyhock

Buying Healthy Plants

Whatever kinds of flowers you buy, do the following:

- Look for bushy, dense, well-branched plants.
- Avoid plants with leggy, lank stems and few leaves.
- Look for healthy green leaves, avoiding plants with yellowed or wilted leaves.
- Avoid plants in pots that seem too small for the overall plant size.
- Avoid plants with bugs, chewed leaves, and sticky patches, which indicate pests. Look under leaves and at stem tips.

HELPFUL TIP

Tip a plant out of its pot to look at its roots before you buy. The roots should fill the pot without crowding or circling around the pot excessively.

Finding Flowers that Thrive

The secret to growing beautiful flowers is simple. Before you buy that first annual or perennial, decide where you want to plant your garden. Then learn about the site's soil and sun or shade conditions. (For details, see "Getting Ready to Garden" on page 12.) Once you know the growing conditions your flowers will be coping with on various parts of your property, use the plant profiles later in this book, plus plant labels at your garden center, in selecting flowers for specific sites.

This strategy ensures success, because the plants don't then need to struggle to survive. It also saves you work, because you don't need to make extra efforts to keep your annuals and perennials healthy and thriving.

Hostas (left and top), epimediums (center), and wild blue phlox all thrive happily in shady spots.

Bulbs for Added Color

Colorful hardy bulbs like daffodils and crocuses are great for adding extra color to flower gardens. Buy these bulbs in fall and plant them in small groups arranged next to your annuals and perennials and annuals. Next spring, they'll add color long before your other flowers begin blooming.

Choosing Garden Flowers

Bold drifts of red and blue salvias with gold rudbeckias create visual impact.
Site: Hollandia Nursery & Garden Center, Bethel, CT

To create a pretty flower bed, use the tips below to make planning easy and foolproof.

Choose a Color Scheme

Pick flowers in colors that all go together. One option is to plant all hot or all cool colors. Reds, yellows, and oranges are hot colors, while blues, purples, pale yellow, and pinks are cool colors.

Look Indoors for Inspiration

Can't decide what colors to choose? Plant annuals and perennials that have flowers in colors that go with your favorite room or even the colors in a favorite rug pattern.

Mix Up Heights and Forms

Combine plants that exhibit different shapes and sizes. Buy taller plants for the back or center of a garden, lower ones for the front edges. Also combine plants with rounded forms and strappy-leaved clumps.

The grassy leaves of spiderworts contrast nicely with large, bold hosta foliage.

Buy in threes. It's tempting to buy one of everything, but for visual impact, buy at least three of each plant you choose. Then arrange them in drifts to create bold blocks of color.

Plan the bloom season. Most annuals bloom all season, but perennials generally bloom for a few weeks. To ensure a constant parade of color, select a mix of perennials that bloom in spring, summer, and fall. Read plant labels and the plant portraits beginning on page 26 for information on bloom season.

Plant and repeat to pull the garden together. Planting a particular plant in more than one spot, or repeating a color in several locations throughout your garden, helps pull a design together. For example, arrange clumps of yellow daylilies along the front of your garden or plant different flowers with red blooms throughout to create a unified look.

Remember your site. Always stick to plants that will thrive in your site's sun and soil conditions. See "Getting Ready to Garden" on page 12 for details.

HELPFUL TIP

A plant's leaves are almost more important than its flowers. Why? Blooms come and go, but leaves are there all season and provide a backdrop for flowers. Choose annuals and perennials that have handsome leaves in a mix of shapes and sizes.

Best Flowers for Attracting Butterflies

I love watching butterflies visit my garden and always look for flowers that attract them. Plants with daisylike flowers are among the best, because they give butterflies a nice landing pad for sipping nectar. Here are some of the best butterfly flowers I have found. All are listed in the Plant Portraits section beginning on page 26.

Zinnias are excellent butterfly plants.

Butterfly weed

Coreopsis

Echinaceas

Marigolds

Petunias

Phlox

Salvias

Scabiosas

Sedums

Shasta daisies

HELPFUL TIP

Like butterflies, hummingbirds enjoy visiting petunias, phlox, salvias, geraniums, and zinnias. To attract hummingbirds, you can also plant daylilies, snapdragons, columbines, foxgloves, bee balm, pinks, and hostas.

When You Get Home

Protect new plants from sun and wind until planting.

It's important to give your new plants extra TLC when you get them home. Drying out to the point of wilting causes root and shoot damage, and too much sun can cause leaf scorch. Use these tips to keep your new plants healthy.

- Set them in a shady spot protected from wind. A site on the north side of the house or under shrubbery is fine.

- Check the weather, and keep annuals indoors in a cool (45 to 55°F) spot until nighttime temperatures do not drop below freezing.

- Water thoroughly. If the water seems to be flowing through the pot without wetting the soil, set pots in a container of water and let them soak for a few minutes.

- Check plants daily and water whenever the soil seems dry.

HELPFUL TIP

If your garden isn't ready to plant, it's often smart to "heel in" plants temporarily. To do this, dig a trench in a shady spot, tip plants out of their pots, and set their root balls into the trench. Cover with soil, and then water. Move plants to their final locations as soon as possible.

Getting Ready to Garden

Use the following tips to make sure your flowers have a big impact and look great for the whole growing season.

Bold clumps of orange daylilies, blue salvia, and yellow yarrow create a big impact.

Concentrate the color. Instead of one plant here and another there, grow flowers in beds and arrange them in drifts or clumps, creating bold blocks of color. Improved soil in planting beds boosts growth and flowering.

Start small. Starting with a small garden minimizes the work it takes to plant and care for your flowers. You can always enlarge your garden later.

Consider containers. If you have poor soil, or can't decide where to plant, buy containers and plant them with a mix of annuals. Keep in mind that large containers are easier to maintain and need less frequent watering than small ones.

Selecting a Site

SAFETY TIP

Before you stick a shovel in the soil, make sure you aren't digging where you could inadvertently cut underground wires or puncture water lines. Contact your local utility company to find out about services that could help you locate underground lines.

To determine soil conditions, dig up a shovel full. No matter what type of soil you have, you'll find information on improving it on pages 16-20.

Gold-leaved hostas add color under deep-rooted trees.

Move your garden farther away from trees and shrubs if the ground is so full of roots you can barely dig. Annuals and perennials can't compete with tree roots and will eventually be crowded out. If you can't garden elsewhere, set large containers or half-barrels of soil on the site (drill holes in the bottom for water drainage), and then garden in containers.

Also use these tips to select a good garden site.

- Locate your garden near an outdoor faucet, so it will be easy to water.
- Avoid sites where family and friends will be tempted to cut through your garden instead of walk around it.
- Pick a spot where you can easily see and enjoy your flowers every day. That makes routine maintenance easy and efficient.

Studying Sun and Shade

Hostas are ideal for sites with partial to full shade.

Marigolds need full sun to flower.

Some flowers only do well in sun, while others need shade. Watch your prospective site for an entire day to decide which of the following categories applies. Then use your sun/shade observations to select the flowers.

Full sun sites receive a minimum of 6 to 8 hours of direct sun per day.

Light shade describes sites that are in shade part of the day, but in sun the rest. Sites with shade in the morning and sun in the afternoon are often suitable for plants that need full sun, while shade-loving plants can grow in spots that receive morning sun and afternoon shade.

Partial shade sites are located under mature trees, where patches of sun and shade (also called dappled shade) reach the ground all day.

Deep shade, or full shade, describes sites that receive little or no direct sun. This can be caused by densely branched trees or evergreens or buildings.

Helpful Tools

Good-quality tools make caring for plants easier. I've found you'll need the following tools to plant and care for a garden.

- Spade or shovel: For turning soil, digging holes, scooping, and moving soil buy a round-point shovel or a flat garden spade.

- Fork: A four-tined garden fork makes loosening and turning soil easy and efficient.

- Common garden rake: A square-headed rake is useful for raking up rocks, and breaking up clods of soil.

- Trowel: This is essential for digging smaller planting holes.

- Gloves: To protect your hands and nails, use a sturdy pair of garden gloves.

In addition, a garden cart or wheelbarrow is handy for moving plants, soil, and garden debris. A bucket is also helpful for various carrying tasks. You also will need hoses, a watering can, and a sun hat!

TIP Try out tools before you take them home. Lift them up, and pretend you are using them for their intended purpose. If they feel too heavy, they probably are.

Planting Your Flowers

Great gardens start with good soil. For this reason, soil improvement tops the list for planting. Fortunately, tasks like adding organic matter can make any garden suitable for growing flowers.

Preparing the Soil

Flowers can't compete with grass roots, so the first step is to remove grass and/or weeds on the site. Once the grass is gone, use the following techniques to build great soil for your flowers.

Slice under the grass with a sharp spade to cut away the roots, but leave as much soil behind as possible.

After plants like these hostas are established, they appreciate side-dressing with compost.

Dig-in organic matter. Spread a 2- to 3-inch layer of compost, leaf mold, or other organic matter over the site. (Check your local garden center for these materials.) Dig the amendment into the soil and turn the soil over a shovel full at a time. Compost and other organic matter help keep soil moist and also let water drain through it, making that magical gardener's combination of moist, well-drained soil. If you don't have much good soil on your site, also spread and dig-in bagged topsoil.

Rake it smooth. Level out the top of your garden with a rake. Your prepared bed should be a few inches higher than the surrounding ground, because you've added organic matter and loosened texture.

Is the Soil Ready?

Good soil has a crumbly texture. If you dig-in soil that is too wet or too dry, you can destroy good texture, making it harder for roots to grow. Before you dig, grab a handful of soil and squeeze it into a ball.

After being squeezed into a ball, if moist soil crumbles easily with the pressure of your finger, it's ready to dig.

If the soil ball remains in a sticky clump, wait a couple of days and test again before digging. If soil crumbles into dust, water it deeply a day or two before you dig.

HELPFUL TIP

Don't ever walk on soil after preparing it. Why? Walking across a newly dug bed compacts the soil, making it much harder for plant roots to grow and harder for water to drain through the soil. Compaction also reduces the amount of air in soil, which roots need to grow.

No-Till Gardens

Layering with biodegradable materials like these is effective in building beds in fall to plant in spring—or in spring for late-summer planting.

All you need to build a great garden is newspaper, organic matter, and some patience. Follow these simple steps.

1. Chop the grass and/or weeds close to the ground.

2. Cover the site with newspapers, 8 to 10 sheets thick.
   Overlap the sheets so no ground is showing. Pile some mulch on each section to keep the newspapers from blowing away.

3. Add layers of compost, chopped up leaves, spoiled hay from barns, and other organic matter. Pile materials 6 to 8 or more inches thick.

4. Top the area with 2 inches of mulch.

5. Wait at least 3 months for the grass and weeds to be smothered and the organic matter to break down. Then plant.

HELPFUL TIP

To create a no-till garden you can plant right away, pile up the layers, then incorporate pockets of topsoil (buy it bagged at your garden center) into each planting hole. After that, mulch and water thoroughly.

Super-Easy Perennials

I always have a hard time selecting perennials at a garden center—at least making choices while staying within my budget! That's because every plant I encounter promises to be prettier than the one I've just chosen.

To help make your selections a bit easier, here is my list of perennials that are the easiest to grow. I've listed eight for sun and eight for shade. All produce a bounty of flowers or handsome foliage for a minimum of care. I've included all of these—plus other favorites—in the Plant Portraits section of this book, beginning on page 26.

Easy for Sun

Coreopsis
Daylilies
Echinaceas
Scabiosas
Siberian iris
Sedums
Shasta daisy
Yuccas

Easy for Shade

Cimicifugas
Epimediums
Ferns
Hellebores
Hostas
Lamiums
Liriopes
Lungworts

Planting Annuals and Perennials

To minimize stress, plant and water each plant separately before starting with the next one.

Once your soil is prepared, use the following steps to plant your flowers.

1. Dig a hole deep enough for the plants's roots and about twice as wide.

2. Tip the plant out of its pot. Hold the pot with two fingers on either side of the main stem.

3. To encourage roots to grow out into the soil, use a knife to make a shallow cut through the surface roots on two or more sides of the root ball.

4. Set the plant in the hole. Make sure the soil surface of the plants is level with, or just slightly higher than, the surrounding soil. Planting too deep causes plants to rot, and planting too shallow causes them to dry out.

5. Fill the hole with soil, making a saucer-shaped depression around the plant so water will run toward it, not away from it. Press the soil firmly around the plant.

Water by flooding the soil around each plant to thoroughly soak it.

Design Check

Before you plant, set pots out on the site where you think you want to plant them. Step back and imagine what they will look like when full grown. Place taller plants toward the back, and shorter ones in front. Also make sure they are spaced far enough apart. You'll find height and spacing information on the plant labels and on seed packets.

Sunflower seed leaves with shell still clinging.

Simple from Seed

For a super-easy garden, start with seeds. Zinnias, cosmos, California poppies, cornflowers, or bachelor's buttons, four-o'clocks, sunflowers, and marigolds all are easy from seed. All can be sown directly into garden soil. You can prepare the soil beforehand (see pages 16-20 for directions), but wait until danger of spring frost has passed before sowing.

Sprinkle seeds over prepared soil. Use a watering can with perforated rose to gently sprinkle the seeds daily until plants are established.

Thin seedlings if they are crowded (see seed packets for recommendations). Then mulch and enjoy your garden!

HELPFUL TIP

If possible, plant your garden during cloudy, overcast, even drizzly weather. Clouds and drizzle make it far easier for plants to overcome the shock of being transplanted from their pots into soil.

Caring for Your Garden

To keep your garden thriving, visit it daily. If you attend to tasks every day, it's easy to keep plants thriving with a minimum of work.

Mulching, Watering, and Weeding

Use these tips to keep your garden in topnotch form. Water deeply. Mere sprinkling of the soil surface encourages shallow drought-prone roots. After watering, stick your finger several inches into the soil to make sure water has penetrated into the root zone.

To save water, install soaker hoses. These waterwise hoses leak water all along their length. They run on low water pressure, so turn the faucet only about a quarter turn open and let it run for several hours each time you water.

Feeding

Flowers actually don't need feeding if you add plenty of organic matter to the soil at planting time. If you still want to give your flowers an extra boost, spread a slow-release, organic fertilizer on your beds a few weeks after planting.

Spread mulch

Keep the soil covered with a 1- to 2-inch layer of shredded bark or other mulch to hold moisture in the soil. Mulch also controls weeds.

Weed often

Pulling weeds is easy if you get them when they are still small.

HELPFUL TIP

When spreading mulch, keep it 1 to 2 inches away from plant stems to prevent stem rot and other diseases.

Pinching and Pruning

Use these simple tips to keep your annual and perennial flowers blooming and looking their best!

To encourage branching, bushy growth, and more flowers, remove stem tips with your finger and thumb, or with pruning shears.

Removing spent daylily flowers keeps plants looking neat. On many other plants, removal also encourages new buds to form.

Staking

Let's face it, flopping flowers aren't pretty. Pinching stem tips when plants are young helps keep growth compact and upright. For flowers that need staking, place stakes on 4 or 5 sides of a clump, and wind string around the outside and through the center of the clump. Ideally, install stakes when plants are small before they need staking.

Staking systems like this grow-through support make staking easy.

Tie tall plants to individual stakes using figure-eight knots so stems can move a bit in the wind.

Dividing

Overgrown perennials can die out in the center of the clump. Renew them by digging them up in spring or fall, cutting the clumps into pieces, and replanting.

Use a sharp knife to cut clumps into pieces.

Praying mantids are beneficial insects that hunt pests.

Managing Pests and Diseases

Also watch for signs of pests and diseases on your daily garden walks. Look under leaves and at stem tips for signs of pests, indicated by leaves with yellow speckles, webby stem tips, and patches of sticky honeydew or black mold that signal aphids or spidermites. It's important to remember that most of the insects you see in your garden are either benign or beneficial, meaning they are helping you by eating other pest insects. So if you suspect a problem, take a sample to your local garden center or cooperative extension office, and ask an expert for advice on control steps.

Part 2: Best Flowers for Sun

On the pages that follow, you'll find some of my favorite plants for sunny gardens. Each plant portrait includes a description and the information you need to grow and enjoy the plant. If you pay attention to my recommended sun and soil requirements, you'll be well on your way to success. You'll also find a hardiness rating for each perennial. See the map on page 64 to identify your local Hardiness Zone, and then select plants appropriate for your zone. Based on the information I provide here, you can pick great plants for your garden and get them off to a terrific start.

HELPFUL TIP

If you haven't added organic matter to your soil already, plan to do so at planting time. This improves conditions for roots and also helps keep the soil moist yet well drained.

Achillea

Achillea species **Perennial: Full Sun**

Yarrow 'Summer Mix'

Also called yarrows, these tough, undemanding perennials are prized for their showy, flat-topped clusters of flowers in shades of yellow, white, pink, and orange-red. The handsome fernlike leaves are aromatic.

Height and spread: 2 to 4 feet tall; 2 feet or more wide

Flowering time: Summer

Uses: Combine yarrows with echinaceas, rudbeckias, and other summer flowers.

Hardiness: Zones 3 to 9

How to grow: Give yarrows full sun and average to poor well-drained soil. Rich soil or too much fertilizer causes plants to flop over. Stake clumps as necessary. Dig and divide yarrows in early spring or in fall every 3 to 5 years. Otherwise clumps die out in the center and become less vigorous. Cut off spent flowers to encourage new ones to form.

> **TIP** Cut yarrows for fresh or dried bouquets. To dry them, just hang small bunches upside down in a warm dry place.

Alyssum

Lobularia maritima **Annual: Full Sun to Part Shade**

Alyssum 'Snow Crystal'

Sometimes called sweet alyssum, this dainty, low-growing annual covers the ground with clusters of tiny, fragrant flowers from spring to fall. Flowers come in white, pink, lavender, and purple.

Height and spread: 2 to 4 inches tall; 1 foot wide

Flowering time: Alyssums bloom from spring to fall in the North where the weather remains cool, but stop flowering in hot weather. They bloom from fall to early spring in warm climates. A site with afternoon shade helps plants bloom longer.

Uses: Plant alyssum along the front of a flower garden or along a path as an edging.

Hardiness: Zones 3 to 9

How to grow: Alyssums grow in average soil. Sow seeds outdoors in spring as soon as the soil is no longer frozen, or plant bedding plants in early spring. In mild climates, plant in fall for bloom in winter and early spring.

Amsonia
Amsonia species
Perennial: Full Sun to Part Shade

These easy-to-grow North American natives add clusters of light blue flowers to the garden. Also commonly called blue stars, the individual flowers are star-shaped and are carried in rounded clusters. The plants are bushy with lance-shaped leaves that turn rich yellow in fall.

Height and spread: 1 to 3 feet tall; 2 to 4 feet wide

Flowering time: Late spring to midsummer

Uses: Plant amsonias in flower gardens with perennials like rudbeckias and daylilies.

Hardiness: Zones 3 to 9

Amsonia hubrectii

How to grow: Give amsonias full sun to part shade and average, moist, well-drained soil. Once plants are established, they can withstand some drought. On sites in partial shade, cut plants back after they flower to keep them from flopping. Divide plants as needed in spring or fall.

Baptisia
Baptisia australis
Perennial: Full Sun to Part Shade

This tough, shrub-size perennial produces showy clusters of dark blue flowers in early summer. The flowers of this North American native are followed by blue-black, balloonlike seed pods. The leaves are attractive blue green.

Height and spread: 3 to 5 feet; 2 to 3 feet wide

Flowering time: Early summer

Uses: Plant baptisias toward the back of flower gardens. The foliage makes an attractive backdrop for echinaceas, rudbeckias, and other later blooming flowers.

Hardiness: Zones 3 to 9

Baptisia, False indigo

How to grow: Give baptisia full sun and rich, moist, well-drained soil. Plants are drought tolerant once established. Baptisias are deep-rooted and so do best when not divided or moved. The flowers bloom less in partial shade and are more likely to need staking there.

TIP There also are easy-to-grow baptisias with white or yellow flowers.

Bee Balm
Monarda didyma | Perennial: Full Sun to Part Shade

Bee balm cultivar

As attractive to hummingbirds and butterflies as they are to gardeners, bee balms produce showy, rounded clusters of scarlet or pink flowers. The individual flowers are tube shaped with two lips. Also known as bergamot or Oswego tea, bee balm bears fragrant leaves that can be used to make tea.

Height and spread: 2 to 4 feet tall; 4 or more feet wide

Flowering time: Mid to late summer

Uses: Use bee balms to attract hummingbirds. They also can be used as cut flowers.

Hardiness: Zones 4 to 8

How to grow: Give plants rich, moist, well-drained soil. Powdery mildew can be a problem. So choose a site with good air circulation and buy plants that are mildew resistant. Plants spread quickly. Divide clumps every 2 to 3 years to keep them in check.

Bugleweed
Ajuga reptans | Perennial: Full Sun to Full Shade

Bugleweed

This low-growing ground cover is grown for its pretty spikes of violet-blue flowers plus its ability to spread quickly. The handsome spoon-shaped leaves can be green, burgundy, gray-green, or marked with patches of green, white, and pink.

Height and spread: 4 to 6 inches; 3 feet or more wide

Flowering time: Late spring

Uses: Bugleweed makes a great ground cover along pathways or the front of flower gardens.

Hardiness: Zones 3 to 9

How to grow: Bugleweeds survive in full sun to full shade, but are happiest in partial shade. Give them average to rich soil that is moist but well drained. Dig up individual plants or divide clumps anytime from spring to fall.

> **TIP**
> Keep bugleweed from spreading too far with edging strips, available at garden centers. Otherwise, it easily spreads into lawn areas.

Butterfly weed — *Asclepias tuberosa* — Perennial: Full Sun

Butterfly weed

Tough, undemanding butterfly weed is grown for its showy rounded clusters of orange, orange-red, or yellow flowers—plus its ability to attract butterflies. A North American native, it is especially attractive to monarch butterflies, which lay their eggs on this species.

Height and spread: 2 to 3 feet; 2 feet wide

Flowering time: Midsummer

Uses: Grow butterfly weed in butterfly gardens or low-maintenance flower gardens with echinaceas, rudbeckias, and ornamental grasses.

Hardiness: Zones 3 to 9

How to grow: Give butterfly weed full sun and average well-drained soil. Plants tolerate poor, dry soil as well as sandy conditions. They are deep rooted and thus very difficult to dig and transplant successfully. So pick a permanent site in the garden when you plant. They do not need to be divided regularly.

Celosia — *Celosia* species — Annual: Full Sun

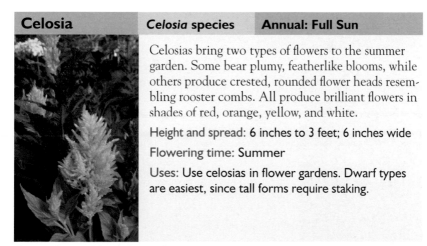

Celosia 'Century Mix' & 'Prestige Scarlet'

Celosias bring two types of flowers to the summer garden. Some bear plumy, featherlike blooms, while others produce crested, rounded flower heads resembling rooster combs. All produce brilliant flowers in shades of red, orange, yellow, and white.

Height and spread: 6 inches to 3 feet; 6 inches wide

Flowering time: Summer

Uses: Use celosias in flower gardens. Dwarf types are easiest, since tall forms require staking.

How to grow: Give celosias full sun and rich, moist, well-drained soil. The plants thrive in heat and humidity. Start with plants and move them to the garden 2 weeks after the last frost date. Keep the soil evenly moist, or plants can become stunted.

TIP: Celosias are outstanding for cut or dried arrangements. Tall forms are best for cutting. Plant them in rows in a vegetable garden to produce a bounty for big bouquets.

Chrysanthemum	*Chrysanthemum* species	Perennial: Full Sun

Commonly called mums, these favorite gift plants bear flowers in many forms, from single daisylike blooms to large double-petaled ones. They can be planted in the garden after their gift days are over.

Height and spread: 1 to 5 feet; 2 to 3 feet wide

Flowering time: Late summer to fall

Uses: Grow mums for late-season color in beds, borders, and containers.

Hardiness: Zones 4 or 5 to 9

Chrysanthemum 'Sheffield Pink'

How to grow: Give chrysanthemums average to rich, well-drained soil. Ideally, plant in spring. Fall-planted mums often do not have enough time to get well established before winter. Mums produced for garden use are better than types sold by florists. Pinch out stem tips (page 23) twice in spring and early summer to encourage bushy growth and more flowers. Do not pinch after July 4th to ensure flowers before frost.

Columbine	*Aquilegia* species	Perennial: Full Sun to Part Shade

Few plants are more appealing than columbines, whose dainty flowers dance on wiry stems above blue-green leaves. Blooms come in nearly all colors including blue, purple, red, yellow, pink, and white. Many flowers have two colors, plus there are double-flowered forms.

Height and spread: 1 to 4 feet tall; 1 foot wide

Flowering time: Late spring to midsummer

Uses: Plant columbines in woodland gardens or informal flower beds.

Hardiness: Zones 3 to 8

Canadian columbine

How to grow: Give columbines rich, moist, well-drained soil. Deep roots make them drought tolerant but difficult to divide or move once established. Plants self-sow their seeds, but seedlings may not resemble their parents.

TIP

To grow columbines from seed, buy seed or collect brown seed capsules from your plants. Sprinkle seeds where you want plants to grow. Move seedlings with a trowel when still small.

Coreopsis   *Coreopsis* species   Perennials, Annuals: Full Sun

Also called tickseeds, coreopsis are easy-to grow annuals and perennials with showy daisylike flowers. The flowers are usually yellow or gold in color and are single or double. Perennial pink coreopsis (C. *rosea*) has rose-pink flowers with yellow centers. Thread-leaved coreopsis (C. *verticillata*), another perennial, is especially popular and features pale yellow to golden flowers. Large-leaved coreopsis (C. *grandiflora*) can be grown as an annual or a perennial. It bears large 1 to 2½ inch flowers. All are wildflowers native to North America.

Height and spread: 1 to 3 feet tall; 2 feet or more wide

Flowering time: Summer to early fall

Uses: Plant coreopsis in sunny beds and borders and wildflower gardens. They also make fine cut flowers.

Hardiness: Zones 3 or 4 to 9

Coreopsis 'Full Moon'   Coreopsis 'Red Shift'   Coreopsis 'Early Sunrise'

How to grow: Full sun and average to rich well-drained soil are all coreopsis needs to thrive. Pink coreopsis also grows in partial shade and likes moist soil. These plants love heat, too, and withstand drought once established. Rich soil can cause flopping. Remove spent flowers to keep plants blooming. Cut thread-leaved coreopsis back by one-half after it flowers to encourage branching and a new flush of blooms. Divide perennials every 2 to 3 years in spring or fall to keep them vigorous.

HELPFUL TIP

Because coreopsis are very attractive to butterflies and other insects, be sure to include them in gardens designed to attract birds and other wildlife. Also, toward the end of the season, stop removing spent flowers and let them go to seed. The seed heads are very appealing to birds in winter.

Centaurea   *Centaurea montana*   Perennial: Full sun to Part Shade

Also called mountain bluet or cornflower, this is a vigorous perennial that produces rich blue flowers in early summer. The flowers look somewhat like thistles, with conelike bases and ragged looking petals.

Height and spread: 1½ to 2 feet; 2 feet wide

Flowering time: Early summer

Uses: Plant mountain bluets in informal beds and borders or in wild gardens.

Hardiness: Zones 3 to 8

Centaurea, Mountain bluet

How to grow: Give mountain bluet average to rich well-drained, evenly moist soil. The plants are happiest and spread most quickly in areas where summers are cool. In warm climates they generally need staking. Cut plants to within 6 inches of the ground after the main flush of flowers to encourage reblooming and bushier growth.

Cosmos   *Cosmos* species   Annual: Full Sun

Dependable, showy cosmos are perfect annuals for adding masses of color to the summertime garden. They bear daisylike flowers in shades of pink, maroon, scarlet, yellow, orange, and orange-red. Flowers have yellow centers and may be single or double. Leaves are deeply cut and featherlike.

Height and spread: 1 to 6 feet tall; 1 foot wide

Flowering time: Summer

Uses: Cosmos attract butterflies. Plant them in drifts for bold color in sunny beds and borders and in meadow gardens.

Cosmos 'Sonata'

How to grow: Give cosmos poor to average soil that is moist but well drained. Rich soil yields few flowers and floppy plants. Stake taller selections of cosmos, or buy 1½- to 2-foot dwarf types that don't need staking. Remove spent flowers to encourage reblooming. Grow from seed sown outdoors after danger of spring frost has passed. Cosmos will self sow.

Daylily	*Hemerocallis* **species**	**Perennial: Full Sun**

Versatile and long-lived, daylilies are the backbone of summer flower gardens. They bear showy trumpet-shaped flowers above clumps of strap-shaped leaves. The flowers come in many different colors and sizes, from tiny 1-inch-wide blooms to large 6-inch wide ones. Petals may be ruffled, and many blooms exhibit several colors.

Height and spread: 1½ to 4 feet tall; 3 to 4 feet wide

Flowering time: Late spring to late summer

Uses: Grow daylilies in sunny beds and borders. Shorter dwarf types make handsome edgings or hedgelike plantings. Use large drifts of daylilies as ground covers.

Hardiness: Zones 3 to 10

Daylily 'Hall's Pink'   Daylily 'Winsome Lady'   Daylily 'Rosy Returns'

How to grow: Give daylilies average to rich, evenly moist soil. They tolerate drought and poor soil, but will bloom less there. Very rich soil or too much fertilizer yields abundant foliage but few flowers. Pick off spent flowers and any seedpods that form. Divide the clumps of fleshy roots in early spring or fall when they become crowded, begin to bloom less, or outgrow their space.

HELPFUL TIP

While each daylily flower lasts only a day, you can extend the overall bloom season. First, look for daylilies marked "reblooming," since they produce flowers over a long season. Daylilies also are rated as blooming in early, mid-, and late season. Choose and plant some of each in your garden to enjoy flowers from the beginning of the daylily blooming season to the end. Finally, look for plants with heavily branched bloom stalks, since they produce the most flowers per plant.

Delphinium

Delphinium species   **Perennial: Full Sun to Part Shade**

Delphinium 'Guardian Blue'

Delphiniums are prized for their stately flower stalks in shades of blue, violet, lavender, pink, and white. They produce clumps of maplelike leaves and thrive in regions with cool summer weather. They struggle in summer heat and humidity.

Height and spread: 3 to 6 feet tall; 2 to 3 feet wide

Flowering time: Early and midsummer

Uses: For best effect, arrange delphiniums in drifts of 3 to 5 plants or more.

Hardiness: Zones 3 to 7

How to grow: Delphiniums require very rich, deeply dug soil that is evenly moist (never wet) and well drained. In areas with warm summers, give them a spot that receives morning sun and afternoon shade. Stake flower stalks as they appear because they break easily in the wind. Delphiniums are best grown as short-lived perennials. Replace them every few years.

Echinacea

Echinacea purpurea   **Perennial: Full Sun**

Echinacea 'Kim's Knee High'

These colorful, North American natives are also called purple coneflowers. They bear daisylike flowers with showy petals surrounding a rounded, conelike center. Flowers are 4 to 7 inches wide, with purple-red petals surrounding spiny, orange-brown cones. White-flowered and new yellow-flowered forms are available.

Height and spread: 2 to 5 feet tall; 2 feet wide

Flowering time: Midsummer to fall

Uses: Grow coneflowers in butterfly gardens and meadow plantings. Combine them with phlox, liatris, Shasta daisies, and butterfly weed.

Hardiness: Zones 3 to 9

How to grow: Coneflowers need only average, well-drained soil. Deep roots help them survive heat and drought, but make them difficult to dig and divide, so leave them undisturbed. Coneflowers bloom in light shade, although plants tend to become leggy. The plants self sow, but seedlings may not look like the parent plant.

| **Foxglove** | *Digitalis purpurea* | **Biennial: Full Sun to Part Shade** |

Common foxglove

Grown for their stately, spikes of tubular flowers, foxgloves come in romantic shades of pink, rose-purple, creamy yellow, and white. Spikes arise from a mound of leaves. All parts of this plant are poisonous.

Height and spread: 2 to 6 feet tall; 1 ½ to 2 feet wide

Flowering time: Early summer

Uses: Plant foxgloves in drifts of 3 to 5 or more plants for best effect.

Hardiness: Zones 4 to 8

How to grow: Give foxgloves rich, moist, well-drained soil. From Zone 7 south, plant in a site that is shaded in the afternoon. Water regularly during dry weather. As biennials, foxgloves produce basal leaves the first year and flowers the second. Buy plants, or start seeds indoors early for bloom the first year.

TIP
Foxgloves self sow. To encourage this, remove all but one flower stalk once blooms fade.

| **Gaillardia** | *Gaillardia* species | **Perennials, Annuals. Full Sun** |

Gaillardia 'Portola Giant'

Commonly called blanket flowers, these are tough, easily satisfied wildflowers native to North America. They bear daisylike blooms in shades of red, maroon, yellow, and orange.

Height and spread: 2 to 4 inches tall; 1 foot wide

Flowering time: Early summer to fall

Uses: Grow blanket flowers to attract butterflies or as cut flowers. Plant them with coreopsis and butterfly weed.

Hardiness: Zones 3 to 8

How to grow: Give gaillardias average to rich, well-drained soil. They tolerate poor, sandy soil. Cautions: Very rich soil causes floppy stems, and wet soil causes root rot. Pick spent flowers to encourage reblooming. Divide perennial blanket flower (*G.* × *grandiflora*) every 2 to 3 years to keep plants vigorous. Start annual blanket flower (*G. pulchella*) from seed sown indoors or out. Because the seeds need light to germinate, lightly press them onto the soil surface.

Gazania

Gazania species | **Annual, Tender Perennial: Full Sun**

Native to tropical Africa, gazanias produce their daisy flowers in an array of rich, hot colors including orange, gold, yellow, bronze, pink, red-orange, and white. Many feature petals with contrasting stripes or bands. The flowers close in cloudy weather and at night.

Height and spread: 8 to 12 inches tall; 8 to 10 inches wide

Flowering time: Summer to fall

Uses: Gazanias are great in containers, in rocky gardens, and for edging in raised beds.

Gazania 'Daybreak XP Mixture Improved'

How to grow: Plant gazanias in poor to average, very well-drained soil. They tolerate heat, drought, and salt spray. Roots rot in rich or constantly wet soil or in areas with wet, humid summers. Remove spent flowers to encourage rebloom.

> **TIP** Grow gazanias as perennials from Zone 8 south. In the North, grow them as annuals or dig them in fall and overwinter them indoors.

Geranium

Pelargonium species | **Annual, Tender Perennial: Full Sun**

The rounded flower clusters of geraniums are highly popular in window boxes and other containers. Blooms come in shades of red, pink, and white above handsome, nearly round leaves. Some types have multicolored leaves. Ivy geraniums have cascading stems. Scented geraniums feature fragrant foliage.

Height and spread: 1 to 2 feet tall; 1 foot wide

Flowering time: Early summer to frost

Uses: Geraniums are ideal for sunny beds and borders or containers. Their flowers attract hummingbirds.

Geranium 'Designer Series'

How to grow: Give geraniums rich, well-drained soil. They'll tolerate light shade, but bloom less there. In areas with very hot summer temperatures, a site that receives shade in the afternoon is best. Pinch plant stems to encourage branching and bushy growth (page 23).

> **TIP** Geraniums are easy to keep over winter. Bring containers indoors in fall and keep the soil barely moist in a cool (50°F) bright room.

Hibiscus

Hibiscus moscheutos | Perennial: Full Sun

Also called common rose mallow, this shrub-size native wildflower brings huge 8 to 10-inch wide flowers to the garden. The funnel-shaped blooms come in red, pink, and white.

Height and spread: 4 to 8 feet tall; 3 feet or more wide

Flowering time: Summer

Uses: Include hibiscus in sunny flower gardens or plant it with shrubs or foundation plants for added color.

Hardiness: Zones 5 to 10

Rose mallow (*Hibiscus moscheutos*)

How to grow: Give hibiscus rich, well-drained soil. Evenly moist soil is best. Plants come up late in spring, so mark their location with stakes to avoid digging into them by mistake. Compact forms ranging from 2 to 3 feet tall also are available. Hibiscus are hard to divide. Leave them undisturbed.

TIP

Hibiscus is surprisingly easy from seed. Sow seeds indoors in winter for flowers the first year.

Hollyhock

Alcea rosea | Biennial, Perennial: Full Sun

Old-fashioned hollyhocks are grown for their erect spikes of funnel-shaped flowers carried above large mounds of lobed leaves. The 2 to 4-inch blooms may be single or double and come in shades of yellow, pink, red, maroon, and white.

Height and spread: 4 to 8 feet tall; 2 feet wide

Flowering time: Early- to midsummer

Uses: Plant hollyhocks along fences and buildings or at the back of flower borders. Drifts of several plants are most effective.

Hardiness: Zones 3 to 9

Hollyhock

How to grow: Give hollyhocks average well-drained soil. They bloom best in full sun but tolerate light shade. Plant in a site protected from wind, or stake plants to keep them erect. Dwarf forms, from 2 to 3 feet tall, seldom need staking. Hollyhocks are short-lived perennials. Replace them every 2 to 3 years. But they do self sow.

Iris   *Iris* species   Perennials: Full Sun to Part Shade

Showy colorful flowers, handsome strap-shaped leaves, and undemanding constitutions make iris welcome additions to flower gardens.
Bearded irises produce 4 to 8-inch-wide blooms in all colors of the
rainbow. Japanese iris (*I. ensata*) and Siberian iris (*I. sibirica*) produce
equally showy blooms in shades of violet-blue, purple, and white.
Japanese irises also come in pink and maroon, while Siberians also
come in dazzling blue and yellow.

Height and spread: 1 to 3 feet tall; 2 feet or more wide

Flowering time: Bearded and Siberian iris, late spring to early
summer; Japanese iris, early to midsummer.

Uses: Grow bearded and Siberian iris in sunny beds and borders.
Japanese and Siberian irises are ideal for planting around ponds with
moisture-loving ferns and hostas.

Iris 'Oklahoma Bandit'   Japanese iris 'Kagari Bi'   Siberian iris

How to grow: Give bearded iris average to rich well-drained soil. Midsummer to early fall is the best time to plant or to divide clumps. Dig and divide
clumps every 3 years in midsummer. Set them back in the soil with the fleshy
rhizomes (roots) halfway above ground. Stake flower stalks. Cut back leaves
and rake beds clear of debris in fall to prevent pests and diseases.
Hardiness: Zones 3 to 9

Plant Japanese iris in full sun or partial shade. They need rich soil that is constantly moist in spring and summer; drier in fall and winter. Divide clumps in
early spring or fall every 3 to 4 years. Hardiness: Zones 4 to 9

Plant Siberian iris full sun or light shade. They grow in well-drained, evenly
moist, or constantly wet soil. Divide Siberian irises in early spring or fall, but
only when they are so crowded they begin to stop blooming.
Hardiness: Zones 2 to 9

| **Lavender** | *Lavandula angustifolia* | **Perennial: Full Sun** |

Above all, lavenders bring fragrance to the garden. Both the gray-green, needlelike leaves and the flowers are wonderfully aromatic. The tiny lavender, dark purple, pale pink or white flowers are borne in dense spikes.

Height and spread: 2 to 3 feet tall; 3 to 4 feet wide

Flowering time: Summer

Uses: Plant lavenders along pathways or around patios where you can enjoy their fragrance.

Hardiness: Zones 5 to 9

Lavender 'Madeline Marie'

How to grow: Give lavender any well-drained soil. Wet conditions lead to root rot and death. Best in full sun, they tolerate very light shade, although shade causes leggy plants with fewer flowers. Established plants tolerate drought. Trim plants annually in spring to keep them bushy.

> **TIP** Use lavender flowers in fresh or dried arrangements. To dry them, hang small bunches in a dark, dry spot for several weeks.

| **Lobelia** | *Lobelia erinus* | **Annual: Full Sun to Part Shade** |

Also called edging lobelia, this pretty annual brings masses of tiny purple, pink, magenta, or white flowers to the garden. Plants can be upright or cascading. Edging lobelias are tender perennials native to South Africa, although they are primarily grown as annuals in North America.

Height and spread: 4 to 9 inches tall; 6 inches wide

Flowering time: Early summer to frost

Uses: As their name suggests, edging lobelias are wonderful for edging flower gardens. They also are outstanding for containers where they are especially pretty draping over the edges.

Lobelia 'Riviera Mix'

How to grow: Plant edging lobelia in rich, evenly moist soil. From about Zone 7 south, partial shade is best, especially if you give them a spot that is shaded during the afternoon. Water regularly during dry weather, since plants are not drought tolerant.

Marigold   *Tagetes* species   Annuals: Full Sun

Easy-to-grow marigolds belong in every sunny garden. They bear or-ange, gold, yellow, red-brown, maroon, and even creamy white blooms. The flowers may be single or double, and size varies according to the type. French marigolds are compact—under 1 foot tall—and feature 1 to 2 inch flowers. African or American marigolds produce 4 to 5-inch blooms on plants to 3 feet tall. Tripliod marigolds are a cross between the two. They have 2 to 3-inch flowers on 1-foot plants. They are espe-cially tolerant of stress, and bloom even in very hot weather.

Height and spread: **6 inches to 3 feet; 1 to 1½ feet wide**

Flowering time: **Early summer to frost**

Uses: **Grow marigolds with sun-loving annuals like zinnias. Shorter types are great for edging beds and also for containers. Plant extra African or American types so you can pick them for indoor bouquets.**

Marigold 'Durango Red'   Marigolds left to right: 'Disco Flame'   Marigold 'Starfire'
                          'YellowBoy' & 'LittleHero'

How to grow: **Give marigolds a site with average, well-drained soil. In areas with hot summers, a site that receives afternoon shade is best. Plants tolerate drought, but bloom best with regular watering. Pinch new plants at plant-ing time to encourage bushy growth and more flowers. French marigolds may stop blooming during hot weather. Cut them back and they will resume blooming when cooler weather arrives. Removing spent flowers encouragess new ones to form.**

HELPFUL TIP

Marigolds are very easy annuals to grow from seeds. Sow two or three seeds per pot 6 to 8 weeks before the last spring frost date. Keep them evenly moist in a sunny 70°F room. Or sow seeds directly in the garden after danger of frost.

Morning Glories   *Ipomoea* species   Annuals, Tender Perennials: Full Sun

Morning glories are beloved, old-fashioned vines with colorful, trumpet-shaped flowers that open in the morning. Blooms come in rich blue, pink, maroon, purple-blue, and white. Red-flowered morning glories, plus closely related cypress vine and cardinal climber, are especially attractive to hummingbirds. Closely related cousins, moon flowers open their fragrant flowers at night.

Height and spread: 6 to 10 feet tall; several feet wide

Flowering time: Summer

Uses: Train morning glories to climb trellises, strings attached to a fence. or deck or porch railings.

Morning glory 'President Tyler'

How to grow: Give plants average, moist, well-drained soil. They need strings or trellises to climb. Install these before you plant. Morning glories are best grown from seeds sown directly in the garden. Two weeks after the last spring frost date, soak seeds in water for 24 hours before sowing. Germination takes 1 to 3 weeks.

Nasturtium   *Tropaeolum majus*   Annual: Full Sun

Nasturtiums are climbing or mounding plants with nearly round leaves and showy spurred flowers in shades of red, orange, yellow, and cream.

Height and spread: Climbing types grow to 8 feet tall, mounding types to 1½ feet tall and to 2 wide.

Flowering time: Summer to fall

Uses: Let nasturtiums trail over walls or rocks, use them as edging plants, or plant them in containers.

Nasturiums

How to grow: Give nasturtiums poor, well-drained soil. Rich soil yields foliage but few flowers. You can buy nasturtiums but they are easy to grow from seed. Just plant the seeds outdoors one week after the last spring frost date. Install strings or trellises for climbers before you plant.

TIP
Nasturtium flowers and foliage are edible and have a pleasant spicy taste. Pick leaves and blossoms from flower beds or, for a steady supply, grow extra plants in your vegetable garden.

Pansies

Viola × *wittrockiana* **Annual, Biennial: Full Sun to Part Shade**

Pansy hybrid 'Antique Shades'

The charming, rounded blooms of pansies signal spring. From Zone 7 south, plant them in fall for bloom in late winter and early spring. The 2½ to 4-inch-wide flowers come in all colors of the rainbow. Some are solid colors, but many more have cute, face like blotches in contrasting colors.

Height and spread: 6 to 9 inches tall; 9 to 10 inches wide

Flowering time: Late winter or spring

Uses: Plant pansies as edgings, combine them with spring bulbs, or grow them in containers.

How to grow: Pansies need rich, moist, well-drained soil. In hot climates, pansies do best if they have afternoon shade. Pick flowers often to encourage reblooming. Plants die out by midsummer in hot climates.

TIP | Johnny-jump-ups have smaller, pansylike flowers on 5-inch plants. Grow them like pansies. Where they're happy, they'll self sow.

Peony

Paeonia hybrids **Perennial: Full Sun**

Peony 'Bev'

Peonies are prized for their showy, often fragrant flowers that range from single to double. The 4 to 8-inch blooms come in pinks, creams, reds, and whites.

Height and spread: 2 to 3 feet tall; 3 to 4 feet wide

Flowering time: Late spring to early summer

Uses: Plant peonies in beds and borders or along walkways.

Hardiness: Zones 3 to 8

How to grow: Peonies need average to rich well-drained soil. They are long lived and best left undisturbed once planted, so select their site carefully. In Zones 7 and 8, give them a site that's shady in the afternoon. Plant bare-root peonies in fall, container-grown plants in spring or fall. Look for buds on the roots and set plants with the buds no more than 2 inches below the soil surface. Deep planting prevents flowering.

Petunia

Petunia 'Strawberry Daddy' & 'Daddy Blue'

Petunia × *hybrida*   **Annual, Tender Perennial: Full Sun**

These popular bedding plants produce single or double trumpets in pink, salmon, violet, red, lavender, and yellow. Flowers may be all one color or marked with contrasting hues.

Height and spread: 10 to 18 inches tall; 1 to 3 feet wide

Flowering time: Early summer to fall

Uses: Grow petunias in beds and borders, as temporary ground cover, and in containers. Hummingbirds and butterflies visit the flowers.

How to grow: Plant petunias in average to rich soil that is well drained. They tolerate light shade as well as poor, even sandy, soil. Water regularly. In midsummer, cut back plants that get scraggly or stop blooming to encourage new growth and flowers into fall.

> **TIP** Calibrachoas, or Million Bells, are grown just like petunias. They have trailing stems and produce masses of 1-inch flowers on 8-inch plants.

Phlox

Garden phlox

Phlox species   **Perennials: Full Sun, Part Shade**

Phlox bear clusters of small, fragrant flowers in pinks, reds, purples, and white. Garden phlox (*P. paniculata*) is best known, but Carolina phlox (*P. carolina*) and wild sweet William (*P. maculata*), both native wildflowers, have fewer disease problems.

Height and spread: 2 to 4 feet tall; 1 to 3 feet wide

Flowering time: Summer to early fall

Uses: Grow phlox with summer-blooming perennials like echinacea, Shasta daisies, and bee balm.

Hardiness: Zones 3 to 9

How to grow: Phlox need rich, deeply dug, moist soil. Water regularly. Afternoon shade is best in warm climates. Stake plants to prevent flopping. Remove flowers to prevent self sowing because seedlings will not look like the parents. Dig and divide the clumps every 2 to 3 years to keep them vigorous.

> **TIP** For spring color, plant easy-to-grow moss phlox (*P. subulata*).

Pinks — *Dianthus* species — Perennials. Full Sun

Charming and old-fashioned, pinks are grown for their blue-green leaves and dainty flowers that often have a spicy scent. The petals have fringed or ragged edges that look as if they were trimmed by pinking shears. Flowers come in shades of pink, plus red, maroon, and white. The plants are low growing or mound shaped.

Height and spread: 3 to 12 inches tall; 1 to 2 feet wide

Flowering time: Late spring to midsummer

Uses: Combine pinks with sedums, lavender, columbines, and moss phlox.

Hardiness: Zones 3 to 9

Dianthus amurensis 'Siberian Blue'

How to grow: Pinks need average soil that is well drained and evenly moist to dry. Well-drained soil is especially important in winter. A site with shade in the afternoon is best from Zone 7 south. Removing spent flowers encourages reblooming. Divide clumps every 2 to 3 years to keep them vigorous.

Rudbeckia — *Rudbeckia* species — Biennials, Perennials. Full Sun

Showy, hot-colored flowers, produced in abundance, make rudbeckias outstanding additions to any sunny garden. Also called coneflowers, they bear daisylike flowers with petals in shades of orange, gold, yellow, bronze, rusty orange, and bronze. Blooms may be single or double.

Height and spread: 1½ to 3 feet tall; 1½ feet wide

Flowering time: Summer to early fall

Uses: Plant rudbeckias with sedums, echinaceas, yuccas, and ornamental grasses.

Hardiness: Zones 3 to 9

Rudbeckias: 'Cappuccino' foreground

How to grow: Average to rich soil suits rudbeckias. Evenly moist conditions are best, but plants tolerate drought once established. Most do not need staking, but tall 6 to 9- foot rudbeckias, including giant coneflower, may need to be staked. Plants do not need dividing regularly and are very low maintenance once established. Black-eyed Susans or gloriosa daisies are biennials or short-lived perennial rudbeckias. Replace them every year.

Salvia

Salvia species

Annuals, Tender Perennials, Biennials, Perennials: Full Sun to Part Shade

Gardeners grow many different salvias (sages). All produce showy spikes of two-lipped, tubular flowers. Flowers come in shades of blue, violet, purple, mauve, scarlet, pink, and white. Many also have leaves that are fragrant when crushed or bruised.

Height and spread: 2 to 6 feet tall; 1 to 2 feet wide

Flowering time: Summer to frost

Uses: Salvias are great for summer flower gardens, regularly visited by hummingbirds and butterflies.

Hardiness: Zones 4 to 8

Pineapple-scented sage

How to grow: Give salvias rich, moist, well-drained soil. From Zone 7 south, a site with afternoon shade is best. Pinch plants (page 23) to encourage bushy growth and more flowers.

TIP Most salvias are not winter hardy, but you can take cuttings in late summer. Root them in equal parts vermiculite and perlite. Keep plants in a cool (60°F) sunny spot indoors and replant in spring.

Scabiosa

Scabiosa speciess

Annuals, Perennials: Full Sun

Whether you call them scabiosa, pincushion flower, or sweet scabious, these are long-bloomers with handsome rounded flowers in shades of lavender, pink, white, yellow, and purple. The rounded, somewhat daisylike flowers resemble pincushions, actually clusters of small flowers on tall stems above mounds of leaves.

Height and spread: 2 to 3 feet tall; 10 inches to 2 feet wide

Flowering time: Summer to fall

Uses: Combine scabiosas with lavender and daylilies. Butterflies and hummingbirds visit the flowers, which also are good for cutting.

Hardiness: Zones 3 or 4 to 9

Scabiosa 'Pink Diamonds'

How to grow: Give scabiosas average well-drained soil. They can't tolerate constantly moist soil, especially in winter. Afternoon shade is best from Zone 7 south. Remove spent flowers to encourage reblooming. Divide perennials in spring if they get too big or outgrow their space.

Sedum | *Sedum* species | Perennials: Full Sun

Also called stonecrops, sedums are equally at home in flower gardens or as ground covers. Clump-forming types like popular 'Autumn Joy' bear rounded flower heads that turn from green to red-brown. Sedums also bear magenta, pink, white, or yellow flowers. The tiny starry flowers are carried in dense showy clusters. Leaves are fleshy and rounded or oval.

Height and spread: 1 inch to 3 feet; 3 or more

Flowering time: Summer to fall

Uses: Combine clump-forming sedums with echinaceas, rudbeckias, yuccas, and ornamental grasses. Plant ground covers as edgings or on rocky sites.

Hardiness: Zones 3 to 9

Sedum 'Autumn Joy'

Sedum ruprestre 'Angelina'   Sedum 'Autumn Fire'

How to grow: Give sedums average to rich well-drained soil. They also tolerate poor, dry soil. Constantly moist or wet soil causes root rot and death. Divide clump-forming types in spring, ground-cover types in spring or fall.

| **Shasta daisy** | *Leucanthemum × superbum* | **Perennial: Full Sun** |

These popular garden flowers bring masses of daisy flowers to the garden. Typically the flowers have white petals with yellow centers, but newer introductions feature creamy yellow petals as well. Blooms may be single, semidouble, or double and range from 2 to 5 inches across.

Height and spread: 1 to 4 feet tall; 2 feet wide

Flowering time: Early summer to early fall

Uses: Grow Shasta daisies with daylilies, lavender, sedums, and salvias.

Hardiness: Zones 3 or 4 to 8

Leucanthemum 'Ice Star'

How to grow: Give these easy-to-grow perennials average to rich soil that is well drained. They also tolerate light shade and dry, sandy soil. Plants may be short-lived in hot climates. Divide clumps every 2 to 3 years.

TIP
For an unlimited supply of flowers for bouquets, plant a row of Shasta daisies in the vegetable garden!

| **Snapdragon** | *Antirrhinum majus* | **Annual: Full Sun** |

Beloved by children and adults alike, snapdragons feature spikes of fragrant, two-lipped flowers that open and close when you pinch the back of the bloom. Double-flowered snapdragons are available, too, but they do not "snap." They come in every color except true blue, and selections feature either solid-color or bicolor blooms.

Height and spread: 6 inches to 3 feet; 6 inches wide

Flowering time: Summer

Uses: Plant with summer annuals like marigolds and zinnias. Grow tall snapdragons as cut flowers. Dwarf selections are handsome in containers.

Snapdragon 'Rocket Mix'

How to grow: Plant snapdragons in rich, well-drained soil. Taller types require staking to keep the bloom stalks erect. To avoid need for staking, plant 6- to 8-inch dwarf selections. From Zone 7 south, plant snapdragons outdoors in fall and mulch them deeply with chopped leaves over winter for spring bloom.

Sunflower	*Helianthus annuus*	**Annual: Full Sun**

Vigorous and fast-growing, sunflowers have large, rough-textured, heart-shaped leaves and wide daisy-type flower heads that may be anywhere from 4 to 12 inches wide. Flowers can be single to double and come in shades of yellow, gold, maroon, and bronze.

Height and spread: 1 to 15 feet tall; 1 to 2 feet wide

Flowering time: Summer

Uses: Plant dwarf sunflowers with zinnias or other sun-loving annuals. Sunflowers make wonderful cut flowers and attract butterflies.

Burpee Mammoth Sunflower

How to grow: Give sunflowers average, moist, well-drained soil. While they are sometimes available as plants, sunflowers are easy to grow from seed. Just prepare the soil; then after the last spring frost date, sow seeds directly into the soil.

> **TIP** Tall plants can be hard to incorporate in a landscape. For best effect plant them at the back of flower borders, or along fences or buildings.

Veronica	*Veronica* species	**Perennials: Full Sun, Part Shade**

Also known as speedwells, these are vigorous easy-to-grow perennials that produce showy, bottle-brush-type flower spikes. The tiny individual flowers come in shades of blue, violet-blue, pink, and white. In addition to clump-forming speedwells for beds and borders, there also are mat-forming ones that make good ground covers.

Height and spread: 3 inches to 4 feet; 1 to 3 feet wide

Flowering time: Late spring to early summer

Uses: Combine speedwells with daylilies, coreopsis, and Shasta daisies.

Hardiness: Zones 3 or 4 to 8

Spike speedwell 'Royal Candy'

How to grow: Give speedwells average to rich moist-but-well-drained soil. They cannot tolerate constantly moist soil, which causes root rot especially in winter. Water during dry weather. Stake taller types and cut them back after the flowers fade. Divide clumps in spring or fall every 3 to 4 years.

Vinca

Vinca 'Stardust Orchid'

Catharanthus roseus

Annual, Tender Perennial: Full Sun to Part Shade

Also called rose or Madagascar periwinkle, these tough, sturdy tender perennials bear flat-faced trumpet-shaped flowers with 5 petals. Blooms come in shades of pink or white, and most have a central "eye" in a contrasting color.

Height and spread: 1 to 2 feet tall and wide

Flowering time: Summer to frost

Uses: Plant vinca in drifts for splashes of color. Used en masse they make fine temporary ground covers.

How to grow: Vincas need average to rich, evenly moist soil that is well drained. Once established, they tolerate heat and humidity. Pinch plants early in the season to encourage branching and more flowers.

TIP Vincas are easy to save indoors from year to year. Pot-up plants in fall and keep them in a cool (60 to 65°F) sunny spot over winter.

Yucca

Yucca 'Golden Sword'

Yucca filamentosa | Perennial: Full Sun

Few perennials are as tough as yuccas. The plants produce a clump of strap-shaped evergreen leaves. In summer, an erect 5 to 6-foot tall flower stalk emerges bearing creamy white, 2-inch-wide flowers. While green-leaved forms are common, look for yuccas with variegated leaves striped with yellow or white.

Height and spread: foliage mound, 2½ feet tall; 2 to 3 feet wide.

Flowering time: Summer

Uses: Combine yuccas with echinaceas, rudbeckias, sedums, and ornamental grasses.

Hardiness: Zones 4 to 10

How to grow: Yuccas grow in dry, sandy soil or rich, evenly moist conditions. They need well-drained soil. Remove the flower stalks when they fade. Clumps are composed of many crowns, so also remove the crown that produced the flowers, since it will die and be replaced by new growth. Yuccas can be left undivided for years.

Zinnia   *Zinnia*   Annuals: Full Sun

Few annuals are as popular and easy to grow as zinnias. They come in a wide range of colors, including magenta, red, orange, pink, yellow, gold, cream, and even green. The flowers can be single and daisylike or so double they are nearly round. Blooms range from 1½ to 5 inches wide.

Height and spread: 6 inches to 4 feet; 1 to 2 feet wide

Flowering time: Summer

Uses: Plant zinnias with salvias and other sun-loving annuals or perennials. The flowers attract butterflies and hummingbirds. Tall cultivars make wonderful cut flowers, while dwarf types are excellent for edgings.

Zinnia 'Purple Prince'   Zinnia 'Profusion Orange'   Cactus-flowered zinnia cultivar

How to grow: Give zinnias average to rich, well-drained soil. A site with good air circulation helps reduce problems with powdery mildew. In areas with hot, humid summers, look for newer zinnias developed for their disease resistance. Zinnias are available as bedding plants, but many more colors and sizes are available from seed. Fortunately, they are very easy to grow from seed. Just prepare the soil and plant after the last frost date. For continued bloom, plant new crops of seed every 2 to 3 weeks from late spring to midsummer. In the South, sow seeds in midsummer for bloom into the fall and early winter. Pinch plants to encourage branching, bushy growth and more flowers. Tall zinnias may need staking.

HELPFUL TIP

Newer disease-resistant hybrid zinnias, including 'Profusion Orange', above, are 1- to 2-foot-tall annuals with flowers in shades of gold, orange, maroon, or white. Also called narrow-leaved or Mexican zinnias, they tolerate heat and humidity, making them great additions for summer gardens.

More Great Flowers for Sun

In my garden, more plants are always a good thing. I am always adding new treasures to my flowerbeds, and I am sure you will want to as well. Here are a few more great annuals and perennials I wouldn't want to be without.

Annuals

California poppy

Flowering tobacco

Portulaca

Dwarf morning glory (*Convolvulus tricolor*)
California poppies (*Eschscholzia californica*)
Flowering tobacco (*Nicotiana alata*)
Four-o'clock, Marvel of Peru (*Mirabilis jalapa*)
Larkspur, Annual delphinium (*Consolida ajacis*)
Love-in-a-mist (*Nigella damascena*)
Mexican sunflower (*Tithonia rotundifolia*)
Portulaca, Moss rose, Rose moss (*Portulaca grandiflora*)

Perennials

Anemone 'White Splendor'

Geranium 'Johnson's Blue'

Nepeta, Catmint

Anemones (*Anemone* × *hybrida*)
Caryopteris, bluebeard (*Caryopteris* × *clandonensis*)
Cranesbills, Hardy geraniums (*Geranium* species)
Euphorbia, Spurge (*Euphorbia* species)
Helenium, Sneezeweed (*Helenium autumnale*)
Liatris, Gayfeather (*Liatris* species)
Nepeta, Catmint (*Nepeta* species)
Perovskia, Russian sage (*Perovskia atriplicifolia*)
Stokes' aster (*Stokesia laevis*)

Part 3: Best Flowers for Shade

The shady spots in my yard overflow with annuals and perennials. While many of my favorite shade plants bloom, I take extra care to make sure I plant plenty of flowers that feature striking leaves in my shade gardens as well. Leaves that are striped with yellow or white are always handsome, but I also include plants with blue-green and chartreuse leaves.

On the pages that follow, you'll find a host of handsome annuals and perennials for shade.

Astilbe

Astilbe species | **Perennial: Partial Shade to Full Sun**

Handsome fernlike leaves and plumelike flowers make astilbes outstanding garden residents. Blooms come in shades of pink, rose-purple, red, and white.

Height and spread: 1 to 6 feet tall; 2 to 3 feet wide

Flowering time: Summer

Uses: Combine astilbes with hostas, ferns, lungworts, and wild blue phlox.

Hardiness: Zones 4 to 8

Astilbe 'Red Sentinel'

How to grow: Astilbes require rich, constantly moist, well-drained soil. Add plenty of compost to the soil at planting time. Partial shade is best, although astilbes grow in full sun with moist soil in the north. Curled, brown leaf edges indicate the plants are getting too much sun and not enough moisture. Water regularly in dry weather and mulch with compost to keep the soil moist and rich. Dig and divide the clumps every 3 or 4 years in spring or fall to keep them vigorous.

Begonia

Begonia semperflorens

Annual, Tender Perennial: Partial Shade to Full Sun

Also called wax begonias, these popular annuals form mounds of rounded, green or maroon-bronze leaves. The single or double flowers are pink, red, or white.

Height and spread: 8 to 12 inches tall and wide

Flowering time: Early summer to frost

Uses: Grow wax begonias in containers, use them as edging plants, or plant them in drifts throughout the garden.

Wax begonias (from BIG Series)

How to grow: While wax begonias grow in full shade to full sun, they are best in partial shade, especially in the South. Water regularly to keep the soil evenly moist.

HELPFUL TIP

To enjoy wax begonias over the winter, either dig and pot up entire plants or take cuttings. Dip cuttings in rooting hormone like Rootone, and root them in half vermiculite and half perlite. Keep plants on a sunny, cool (60 to 65°F) windowsill.

Bleeding Hearts — *Dicentra* species — Perennials. Light to Full Shade

As their common name suggests, bleeding hearts bear delicate looking flowers that resemble hearts. The flowers dangle on upright stalks above mounds of fernlike leaves.

Height and spread: 1½ to 2½ feet tall; 1 to 2 feet wide

Flowering time: Spring to early summer

Uses: Grow bleeding hearts with hostas, heucheras, and spiderworts.

Hardiness: Zones 2 or 3 to 9

Fringed bleeding heart

How to grow: Bleeding hearts need rich, moist, well-drained soil. Wet soil, especially in winter, leads to root rot and death. Fringed and Western bleeding hearts (*D. eximia* and *D. formosa*) will bloom all summer provided the soil stays evenly moist. Cut common bleeding heart (*D. spectabilis*) to the ground in midsummer when leaves turn yellow. Handle plants carefully, since stems and roots are brittle. Avoid dividing or disturbing them once established.

Cimicifuga — *Actaea* species, *Cimicifuga* species — Perennials: Partial Shade

Commonly called bugbanes or snakeroots, cimicifugas are shrub-size perennials that add late-season flowers to the shade garden. The tiny, creamy white flowers are carried in densely packed, branched spikes above large mounds of deeply cut, handsome fernlike leaves.

Height and spread: 2 to 8 feet tall; 2 to 4 feet wide

Flowering time: Midsummer to fall

Uses: Plant toward the back of shade gardens.

Hardiness: Zones 3 or 4 to 8

Cimicifuga

How to grow: Give cimicifugas rich, moist soil. They will grow in full sun in the North, but require shade, especially in the afternoon, and even moisture in the South. Cimicifugas are slow to become established after planting. Do not dig or divide them.

 For bloom from midsummer to fall, plant American bugbane, black snakeroot, and autumn snakeroot (*C. americana*, *C. racemosa*, and *C. simplex*).

Coleus

Coleus

Solenostemon scutellarioides

Annual, Tender Perennial: Partial Shade

Coleus are prized for their colorful leaves, and there are hundreds of colors and patterns available. Leaves range from huge to tiny, and can have toothed, deeply cut, or frilly edges. Solid color leaves are the exception, and most combine several colors, including green, chartreuse, yellow, maroon, cream, red, and orange. Plants bear spikes of small flowers.

Height and spread: 1 to 3 feet tall and wide

Flowering time: Summer

Uses: Grow coleus in containers and mixed plantings for season-long color.

How to grow: Give coleus rich, moist, well-drained soil. Newer selections tolerate full sun or very light shade. Colors fade in full shade. Pinch stem tips to encourage branching and bushy growth. Water regularly. Remove flower spikes that appear. Don't plant coleus outside until temperatures remain above 50°F. Overwinter plants indoors as you would begonias (page 53).

Epimediums

Epimedium, Barrenwort

Epimedium species

Perennials: Partial Shade, Full Shade

Also called barrenworts or bishop's caps, epimediums bring early season flowers plus outstanding foliage to the garden. They bear tiny flowers in loose, airy clusters on wiry stems before the leaves appear. Plants spread to form broad clumps of handsome compound leaves.

Height and spread: 6 to 16 inches tall; 1 to 2 feet wide

Flowering time: Spring

Uses: Epimediums make excellent ground covers, or combine them with hostas, ferns, and other shade-loving plants.

How to grow: Epimediums prefer rich, evenly moist soil, but established plants tolerate dry shade and withstand competition from most tree roots as well. With rich, constantly moist soil they can grow in full sun. Clumps can grow for years without being divided.

TIP Epimediums need little annual care, but cut back the foliage in late winter so it won't hide the new flowers.

Ferns

Perennials: Partial Shade

Shade gardeners treasure ferns because of the graceful featherlike shapes of their fronds and the delicate texture they add to the garden. Japanese painted fern (*Athyrium niponicum pictum*) features fronds dappled with green, silver, and burgundy. Fronds of autumn fern (*Dryopteris erythrosora*) are bronzy to copper colored in spring. European lady fern (*Athyrium filix-femina*) is an easy-to-grow species with frilly fronds. Christmas fern (*Polystichum acrostichoides*), native to North America, is evergreen. Royal fern (*Osmunda regalis*) and ostrich ferns (*Matteuccia struthiopteris*) can reach 6 feet when growing in rich, moist soil.

Height and spread: 1 to 6 feet tall; 2 to 3 feet or more wide

Flowering time: Does not flower

Uses: Combine ferns with other shade-loving perennials and shrubs. Moisture-loving species are handsome planted beside a pond or in a low-lying area.

Hardiness: Zones 2 to 10, depending on the species.

Japanese painted ferns and heuchera

Japanese painted fern 'Ursula's Red'

Lady fern

How to grow: Give ferns rich, moist, well-drained soil. Autumn fern, ostrich fern, and royal fern also thrive in constantly moist or wet soil. Royal fern also will grow in shallow standing water. Christmas fern also grows in dry conditions once it is established. In spring or fall, dig and divide clumps if they outgrow their space or to make more plants for new sites in the garden.

Foamflower   *Tiarella* species   Perennials: Partial Shade, Full Shade

Foamflowers are grown both for their foliage and their flowers. Plants bear fluffy spikes of tiny flowers above mounds of maplelike leave. Flowers may be creamy white or pink. The leaves may be deeply cut or almost lacy and are often marked with maroon. Some types spread vigorously, while others are clump forming.

Height and spread: 6 to 10 inches tall; 1 to 2 feet wide

Flowering time: Spring

Uses: Grow clump-forming foamflowers along pathways with wild blue phlox, heucheras, and hostas. Use spreaders as ground covers.

Hardiness: Zones 3 to 8

Foamflower

How to grow: Give foamflowers rich, moist, well-drained soil. Their roots rot if the soil stays constantly moist, especially in winter. Dig and divide the clumps in spring or fall if they outgrow their space.

Hellebores   *Helleborus* × *hybridus*
Perennial: Partial Shade to Full Shade

Also called Lenten roses, hellebores are among the earliest perennials to bloom in spring. They produce clumps of leathery evergreen leaves topped by showy clusters of saucer-shaped flowers. Blooms come in white, cream, pink, rose, maroon, and purple-black.

Height and spread: 1 to 1½ feet tall and wide

Flowering time: Late winter to early spring

Uses: Plant hellebores anyplace that would benefit from a splash of spring color.

Hardiness: Zones 4 to 9

Hellebores

How to grow: Hellebores grow in rich, evenly moist, well-drained soil. Once established, they tolerate drought. Cut off the leaves in midwinter so they do not hide the flowers. Move clumps in late spring but only if necessary, since the plants do best if undisturbed.

TIP Look for a planting site protected from the wind to keep the foliage looking its best in wintertime.

Heuchera

Heuchera species

Perennial: Full Sun to Part Shade

Heuchera 'Citronelle'

Gardeners grow two types of heucheras. Coral bells are grown for their airy spires of tiny, bell-shaped flowers in shades of pink, red, and white. Heucheras, which have greenish white flowers, feature showy foliage that can be green chartreuse and marked with silver, maroon, or red purple.

Height and spread: 6 to 12 inches tall; 1½ feet wide

Flowering time: Early summer

Uses: Plant both types along pathways and toward the front of flower or woodland gardens.

Hardiness: Zones 4 to 8

How to grow: Give heucheras and coral bells rich, moist, well-drained soil. Both grow in full sun to full shade, but a site with shade in the afternoon is best. Water regularly during dry weather. Divide clumps every 4 or 5 years to keep them vigorous. Heucheras self sow, but seedlings may not resemble their parents.

Hostas   *Hosta* species

Although hostas bear racemes of trumpet-shaped flowers, it's their leaves that generally make the biggest impact in gardens. While green-leaved forms are available, the types with spectacular variegated leaves add color and interest to the garden all season long. Hosta leaves range from very small to very large. They come in shades of green, gray-green, and blue-green, and may be striped, edged, or blotched with white, cream, or yellow. Variegated cultivars may be more expensive than all-green ones, but they have a much bigger impact in the garden.

Height and spread: 4 inches to 3 feet tall; 9 inches to 4 feet wide

Flowering time: Early summer to early fall

Uses: Hostas make excellent edging or ground covers. Use larger plants in mixed beds or as specimens.

Hardiness: Zones 3 to 8

How to grow: Give hostas rich, moist soil. A site with morning sun and afternoon shade is ideal, and essential from Zone 7 south where leaves can be scorched by sun. Established clumps tolerate drought, but the leaves are biggest and showiest with constant moisture. Hostas can grow in heavy clay or constantly moist soil as well. Low-maintenance plants, hostas take a few seasons to become established but they can be left undisturbed for years without dividing.

TIP

Be sure to remove the bloom stalks after flowering. Hostas will self sow, but the seedlings will have all-green leaves, not showy variegated ones.

Perennials: Partial Shade to Full Shade

Hosta 'Samuri'

Hosta fortunei 'Albomarginata'

Hosta 'Big Mamma'

Impatiens *Impatiens walleriana*

Annual, Tender Perennial: Partial Shade to Full Shade

Impatiens

Also called busy Lizzie and patience plant, impatiens are hardworking, colorful bedding plants for the shade garden. They bear single or double flowers in shades of pink, red, salmon, lavender, white, and orange on mounding plants.

Height and spread: 6 inches to 2 feet tall and wide

Flowering time: Summer to frost

Uses: Plant drifts of impatiens as edgings or to add spots of color to mixed plantings. They are also ideal for containers.

How to grow: Give impatiens rich, moist, well-drained soil. Water regularly in dry weather. To keep impatiens over the winter, dig plants in fall or take cuttings and root them indoors as you would begonias (page 53).

TIP: New Guinea impatiens feature showy flowers and thrive in full to very light shade. Give them the same soil and other care as common impatiens.

Lamium

Lamium 'Beacon Silver'

Lamium maculatum | **Perennial: Partial Shade to Full Shade**

Despite the unattractive common name "spotted dead-nettle," lamiums are pretty garden plants with attractive foliage and flowers. The two-lipped, flowers are borne in small clusters and come in pink, red-purple, or white. The leaves are heart shaped with toothed edges and come in combinations of green, chartreuse, silver, or white.

Height and spread: 8 to 10 inches tall; 2 to 3 feet wide

Flowering time: Summer

Uses: Grow lamiums as ground covers or to add drifts of foliage color to plantings of hostas, heucheras, and other shade-lovers.

Hardiness: Zones 3 to 8

How to grow: Plant lamiums in average to rich, moist, well-drained soil. They also grow in constantly moist soil. Plants spread fairy quickly to form broad mounds. Cut them back in midsummer if they become scraggly. Divide the clumps as needed in spring or fall.

Liriope

Variegated liriope

Liriope muscari | **Perennial: Partial Shade to Full Shade**

Also called lilyturf, this tough, undemanding perennial bears grassy leaves and flower spikes of tiny, lilac, purple, or white above the foliage in fall. Some forms have yellow-striped leaves.

Height and spread: 1 to 1½ feet tall and wide

Flowering time: Fall

Uses: Grow liriope as a ground cover or edging. Create drifts of it in mixed plantings.

Hardiness: Zones 6 to 9

How to grow: Easy to grow, liriope needs rich, well-drained soil to thrive. Plants also tolerate full sun, heat, humidity, drought, and competition with nearby tree roots. Cut or mow the leaves to the ground in late winter to make way for fresh new foliage. Plants self sow. Divide clumps in spring if necessary.

TIP · Creeping lilyturf (*L. spicata*) has narrower leaves and spreads to 2 feet. It is hardy in Zones 5 to 10.

Lungwort

Pulmonaria species | Perennial: Partial Shade to Full Shade

The dainty, bell-shaped blooms of lungworts grace the garden early in the season. Also called pulmonarias and Bethelehem sages, they bear their flowers in small clusters. Blooms come in shades of pink, lavender-blue, violet-blue, or white. They appear before or as the leaves emerge. The leaves are green splashed or marked with silver or white.

Height and spread: 9 to 16 inches tall; 12 to 18 inches wide

Flowering time: Late winter to early spring

Uses: Combine lungworts with hellebores, hostas, bleeding hearts, and epimediums. They are also pretty with spring bulbs.

Hardiness: Zones 4 to 8

Lungwort 'Roy Davidson'

How to grow: Give lungworts rich, moist soil. They thrive in morning sun with afternoon shade as well. Lungworts can grow for years without needing to be divided, but dig them in spring or early fall if necessary. Plants self sow.

Spiderwort

Tradescantia species | Perennial: Partial Shade to Full Shade

Spiderworts produce mounds of strap-shaped leaves topped by clusters of saucer-shaped flowers, each with three petals. Flowers come in violet, lavender-blue, rose-red, pink, and white.

Height and spread: 1 to 2 feet tall; 2 to 3 feet wide

Flowering time: Early to midsummer

Uses: Plant spiderworts with hostas and hellebores in mixed plantings.

Hardiness: Zones 3 or 4 to 9

Spiderwort

How to grow: Plant spiderworts in rich, moist, well-drained soil. They spread quickly in areas with cool summer weather. In hot summer weather they tend to die back and re-emerge in spring. Dig and divide the clumps every 3 to 4 years in spring or fall.

HELPFUL TIP

Spiderworts self sow, but seedlings usually don't resemble their parents. Cut plants to the ground after they flower to keep them neat, encourage reblooming, and reduce self sowing.

Torenia

Torenia fournieri **Annual: Partial Shade**

Also called wishbone flower, torenias feature tubular flowers that have flaring, lobed lips. The 1-inch-long flowers come in shades of violet, purple, pink, magenta, yellow, and white. Plants with solid-color flowers are available, but many have two-toned blooms blotched with contrasting colors.

Height and spread: 12 inches tall; 6 to 9 inches wide

Flowering time: Summer

Uses: Plant torenias with ferns, bleeding hearts, and lamiums. They are attractive in containers. Hummingbirds visit the flowers.

Torenia 'Clown® Mix'

How to grow: Grow torenia in rich, well-drained, moist soil. Plants grown on sites that receive shade in the afternoon tend to have brighter flowers. Move plants to the garden after all danger of frost has passed. Pinch stem tips to encourage branching and more flowers.

 Torenias are ideal for adding color to Southern shade gardens, since they thrive in hot weather.

Turtlehead

Chelone species **Perennials: Partial Shade, Full Sun**

Native North American wildflowers, turtleheads got their unusual name because the tubular, two-lipped flowers resemble the heads of turtles. Flowers are carried on stiff, erect spikes and come in pink, purple, or white.

Height and spread: 1½ to 5 feet tall; 1 to 2 feet wide

Flowering time: Late summer to fall

Uses: Combine turtleheads with hostas, ferns, and cimicifugas. They also are suitable for planting along pond edges or in bog gardens.

Hardiness: Zones 3 to 8

Turtlehead 'Hot Lips'

How to grow: Give turtleheads rich, moist soil that is deeply dug. Add plenty of organic matter to the soil at planting time. Moist soil is especially important in the South, especially if plants are growing in full sun. Turtleheads will grow in wet clay soil as well. Divide the clumps in spring or fall if necessary.

More Great Flowers for Shade

I always try to fill my shady gardens with as many different plants as possible. That way, there's always something to look at in the garden, be it colorful flowers, interesting foliage, or a mix of textures.

Here are some more great plants for shade. Keep in mind that if you have partial shade you can grow many of the plants in "Best Flowers for Sun" as well. Just look at the sun requirements listed in each plant's profile.

Annuals

Browallia, bush violet (*Browallia* species)
Garden balsam (*Impatiens balsamina*)
Plectranthus (*Plectranthus* species)
Polka-dot plant (*Hypoestes phyllostachya*)

Browallia

Lady's mantle

Bergenia 'Bressingham Ruby'

Perennials

Crested iris (*Iris cristata*)
Goat's beard (*Aruncus dioicus*)
Heart-leaved bergenia (*Bergenia* species)
Lady's mantle (*Alchemilla mollis*)
Lily-of-the-valley (*Convallaria majalis*)
Northern sea oats (*Chasmanthium latifolium*)
Primroses (*Primula* species)
Sedges (*Carex* species)
Rodgersia (*Rodgersia* species)
Snowdrop anemone (*Anemone sylvestris*)
Solomon's seal (*Polygonatum* species)
Violets (*Viola* species)
Wild blue phlox (*Phlox divaricata*)
Wild ginger (*Asarum* species)
Wild wood aster (*Aster divaricatus*)

Solomon's seal

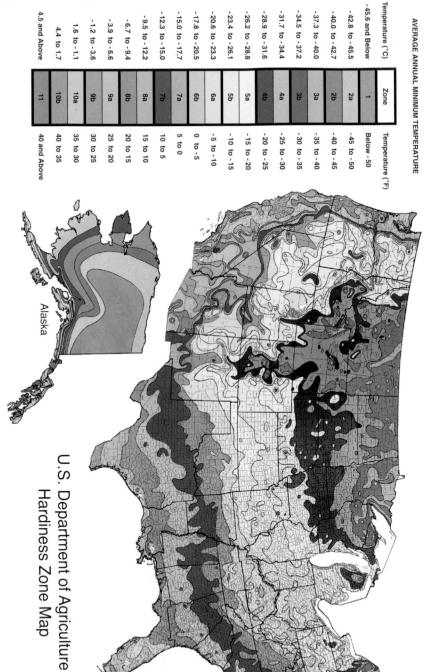

U.S. Department of Agriculture Hardiness Zone Map

AVERAGE ANNUAL MINIMUM TEMPERATURE

Temperature (°C)	Zone	Temperature (°F)
-45.6 and Below	1	Below -50
-42.8 to -45.5	2a	-45 to -50
-40.0 to -42.7	2b	-40 to -45
-37.3 to -40.0	3a	-35 to -40
-34.5 to -37.2	3b	-30 to -35
-31.7 to -34.4	4a	-25 to -30
-28.9 to -31.6	4b	-20 to -25
-26.2 to -28.8	5a	-15 to -20
-23.4 to -26.1	5b	-10 to -15
-20.6 to -23.3	6a	-5 to -10
-17.8 to -20.5	6b	0 to -5
-15.0 to -17.7	7a	5 to 0
-12.3 to -15.0	7b	10 to 5
-9.5 to -12.2	8a	15 to 10
-6.7 to -9.4	8b	20 to 15
-3.9 to -6.6	9a	25 to 20
-1.2 to -3.6	9b	30 to 25
1.6 to -1.1	10a	35 to 30
4.4 to 1.7	10b	40 to 35
4.5 and Above	11	40 and Above

Alaska